IMPROVING
VOCABULARY

for ages 10-11

Andrew Brodie

Introduction

All the activities in *Improving Vocabulary* are specifically designed to promote pupils' knowledge and use of an extensive range of words in their speaking and listening, reading and writing. This six book series provides a structured programme of activities, which will ultimately form invaluable practice for the English grammar, punctuation and spelling test at the end of Key Stage 2.

Research has shown that good use of vocabulary is vitally important for learning and that there is a clear link between a child's level of vocabulary at age five and his or her future success at sixteen or beyond. For good educational progress to be made, children need to experience high-quality language development activities.

Throughout the books, the vocabulary has been carefully selected for the designated age group and progression is also integral to the activities. The activity sheets are differentiated at three levels and are designed to be used by individuals or small groups working with an adult. **Teacher's notes** on each sheet provide guidance on how to get the most from the activity. In general, adults should encourage the children to respond to low-demand questions first before moving on to high-demand questions as they become more confident.

How to use the book and CD-ROM together

The revised National Curriculum Programme of Study for Years 5 and 6 indicates the importance of learning new vocabulary, particularly as part of the reading process. The Programme of Study states that 'teachers should continue to emphasise pupils' enjoyment and understanding of language, especially vocabulary, to support their reading and writing'. It also says 'there will continue to be a need for pupils to learn subject-specific vocabulary'. The Programme of Study for Writing states that pupils should be taught to draft and write by 'selecting appropriate grammar and vocabulary, understanding how such choices can change and enhance meaning'. The activities in this book provide opportunities for practising all of these aspects of the National Curriculum, as well as other important language development skills such as word categorisation.

The book has fifteen Key Activities, which can be projected on to a whiteboard for whole class use and photocopied/printed for display. Sharing the Key Activities either on screen or paper provides lots of opportunities for speaking and listening, for decoding words through a phonic approach, for reading and writing, and for satisfaction and enjoyment in shared success.

For each Key Activity there are three vocabulary sheets at different levels to enable you to differentiate across the ability range in your class. An animal picture at the top of the sheet indicates the level: the cat exercises are at the simplest level; the dog exercises are at the next level and the rabbit exercises are at the most advanced level. You may start off by giving some pupils the cat worksheet and then decide, on the basis of their success, to move them on to the dog worksheet. A similar approach could be taken with the dog and rabbit sheets.

The activity sheets are aimed at the following ability levels:
- Cat activity sheets are for pupils who may need **extra help**.
- Dog activity sheets are for pupils who are **progressing well**.
- Rabbit activity sheets are for **higher ability pupils**.

Contents

Conjunctions

Conjunctions

Conjunctions are used to join phrases or sentences together. They make logical links between ideas.

Teacher's notes

Photocopy and cut out or display the title and simple definition. Explain to the pupils that conjunctions are words that have a special job: they join ideas together. There are several different types of conjunction, including coordinating conjunctions (e.g. and, for), correlative conjunctions (e.g. either … or) and subordinating conjunctions (e.g. because). We also make use of adverbs (conjunctive adverbs) such as however, therefore, nevertheless, moreover, meanwhile - these are often used at the start of a sentence, which follows a related sentence.

Conjunctions

for	and
nor	but
or	yet
so	both ... and
not only ... but also	either ... or
neither ... nor	whether ... or

Teacher's notes

Copy and cut out the words above. Explain to the pupils that conjunctions are words that have a special job: they join ideas together. There are several different types of conjunction, but the activities on this sheet are focused on coordinating conjunctions (e.g. and) and correlative conjunctions (e.g. not only ... but also). However, the emphasis of the work should be on speaking and listening, making use of the conjunctions rather than categorising them into word types. Encourage the pupils to create some oral sentences in which at least one conjunction is used. Note that some words could also be used as prepositions (I had beans for lunch) or as adverbs (I haven't finished yet) but the task is to use them as conjunctions (It's a lovely day for the sun is shining; It's a lovely day yet dark clouds are gathering.) Can the pupils think of a sentence for each of the conjunctions on the sheet? You may need to give them some ideas: Not only is your work brilliant but also it was finished on time!

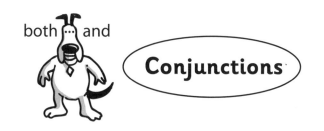

Conjunctions

for	and	nor
but	or	yet
so	both … and	not only … but also
either … or	neither … nor	although
because	when	until
however	therefore	instead
meanwhile	accordingly	nevertheless

Teacher's notes

Copy and cut out the words above. Explain to the pupils that conjunctions are words that have a special job: they join ideas together. There are several different types of conjunction, including coordinating conjunctions (e.g. and), correlative conjunctions (e.g. not only … but also) and subordinating conjunctions (e.g. although). We also make use of adverbs (conjunctive adverbs) such as however, therefore, nevertheless, moreover, meanwhile - these are often used at the start of a sentence, which follows a related sentence. However, the emphasis of the work should be on speaking and listening, making use of the conjunctions rather than categorising them into word types. Encourage the pupils to create some oral sentences in which at least one conjunction is used. Note that some words could also be used as prepositions (I had cereal for breakfast) or as adverbs (I haven't finished yet) but the task is to use them as conjunctions (It's a lovely day for the sun is shining; It's a lovely day yet dark clouds are gathering.) Encourage the pupils to create some oral sentences in which at least one conjunction is used. Can the pupils think of a sentence for each of the conjunctions on the sheet?

Conjunctions

nevertheless

for	and	nor
but	or	yet
so	both … and	not only … but also
either … or	neither … nor	whether … or
although	because	when
until	while	unless
even if	after	before
however	therefore	instead
meanwhile	consequently	thus
otherwise	conversely	hence
furthermore	nevertheless	moreover
meanwhile	accordingly	

Teacher's notes

Copy and cut out the words above. Explain to the pupils that conjunctions are words that have a special job: they join ideas together. There are several different types of conjunction, including coordinating conjunctions (e.g. and), correlative conjunctions (e.g. not only … but also) and subordinating conjunctions (e.g. although). We also make use of adverbs (conjunctive adverbs) such as however, therefore, nevertheless, moreover, meanwhile - these are often used at the start of a sentence, which follows a related sentence. However, the emphasis of the work should be on speaking and listening, making use of the conjunctions rather than categorising them into word types. Encourage the pupils to create some oral sentences in which at least one conjunction is used. Note that some words could also be used as prepositions (I had cereal for breakfast) or as adverbs (I haven't finished yet) but the task is to use them as conjunctions (It's a lovely day for the sun is shining; It's a lovely day yet dark clouds are gathering.) Encourage the pupils to create some oral sentences in which at least one conjunction is used. Can the pupils think of a sentence for each of the conjunctions on the sheet?

Andrew Brodie: Improving Vocabulary for ages 10-11 © Bloomsbury Publishing Plc 2012

Group words

Collective nouns

Teacher's notes

Photocopy and cut out these category title cards to use in conjunction with the activities on the following three worksheets. Explain to the pupils that 'collective noun' is a term that is used instead of 'group word' - this is in itself a valuable example of specialist vocabulary.

Group words

choir	singers	duo	trio	quartet / band
musicians	team	athletes	troupe	dancers / footballers
troop	scouts	guides	cubs	brownies / staff
teachers	album	photographs	stamps	block / flats
army	ants	litter	puppies	kittens / school
porpoises	monkeys	flock	birds	pack / cards

Teacher's notes

Cut out the words and illustrations above and check that the children understand that the activity involves the use of group words and that these are also known as collective nouns. Try to ensure that this is a speaking and listening activity as well as a reading task. Encourage the children to think carefully about each of the items shown on the cards, helping them to match the plural items to the appropriate collective nouns. Note that some items could have several collective nouns associated with them: for example, the words duo, trio, quartet and band could all be used with 'musicians'. Discuss the words troop and troupe - can the pupils decide which to use with dancers and which to use with scouts, guides, brownies or cubs? Ask them to compose some oral sentences, each of which includes a collective noun used appropriately. As an extension activity the pupils could write out a sentence, correctly composed and punctuated.

Andrew Brodie: Improving Vocabulary for ages 10-11 © Bloomsbury Publishing Plc 2012

Group words

Word Bank

porpoises   school   cards   sheep   birds   flock   kittens   tuft   clump

wolves   papers   wheat   monkeys   ants   puppies   hair

army   trees   cluster   diamonds   choir

team   train   camels   pack   footballers

musicians   trio

singers   duo   quartet   band   flats

teachers   album   athletes   troupe   dancers

troop   guides   cubs   brownies

scouts   staff

litter   sheaf   photographs   stamps   block

Insert an appropriate collective noun in each of the gaps below.

a _____ of diamonds   a _____ of dancers   a _____ of photographs

a _____ of wheat   a _____ of guides   a _____ of porpoises

a _____ of wolves   a _____ of ants   a _____ of monkeys

a _____ of musicians   a _____ of footballers   a _____ of hair

a _____ of trees   a _____ of sheep   a _____ of papers

Write two sentences, each of which contains a collective noun for a group.

_____

_____

Teacher's notes

Encourage the children to talk about the group words (collective nouns) listed in the Word Bank, creating oral sentences using these words appropriately with some of the animals, people or objects also listed. Note that some items could have several collective nouns associated with them: for example, the words duo, trio, quartet and band could all be used with 'musicians'. When they are confident in using the words effectively, they can complete the other activities on the sheet.

Group words

Word Bank

porpoises   school   cards   sheep   birds   flock   kittens   tuft   clump

wolves   papers   wheat   monkeys   ants   puppies   hair

army   trees   cluster   diamonds   choir

musicians   team   train   camels   pack   footballers

singers   trio   quartet   band   flats

teachers   duo   athletes   troupe   dancers

troop   album   guides   cubs   brownies

litter   scouts   sheaf   photographs   stamps   block   staff

Match all the collective nouns from the Word Bank with appropriate animals, people or objects. Can you think of other collective nouns?

_____   _____   _____
_____   _____   _____
_____   _____   _____
_____   _____   _____
_____   _____   _____
_____   _____   _____
_____   _____   _____
_____   _____   _____
_____   _____   _____
_____   _____   _____
_____   _____   _____
_____   _____   _____
_____   _____   _____

Teacher's notes

Ask the children to talk about the group words (collective nouns) listed in the Word Bank, creating oral sentences using these words appropriately with some of the animals, people or objects also listed. Note that we are not seeking for children to know and remember all of the collective nouns. Instead, we are trying to encourage them to consider why certain vocabulary may have been chosen.

    Andrew Brodie: Improving Vocabulary for ages 10-11 © Bloomsbury Publishing Plc 2012

Word sorting: English, maths, science

Non-fiction

Information

English

Maths

Science

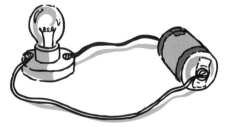

Teacher's notes

Photocopy and cut out the Non-fiction or Information headings and the category title cards to use in conjunction with the activities on the following three sheets. This type of categorisation activity can be very challenging for some children. All of the vocabulary listed will be of direct relevance to the pupils' work, now or in the future.

Word sorting:
English, maths, science

prefix	biography	proverb	suffix	preposition	autobiography
mnemonic	paragraph	biology	biologist	physics	chemistry
habitat	micro-organism	gravity	friction	magnetism	experiment
sphere	spherical	digit	factor	prime	average
median	probability	perimeter	perpendicular	dictionary	pair of compasses
circuit	electricity	mean	circumference	parallelogram	grammar

Teacher's notes

Cut out the words and illustrations above and use them in conjunction with the category title cards from page 13. Ask the children to sort the words: which words could be found in a book about English, which in a book about maths and which could be found in a science book? Could any of the words appear in more than one of the books? Could any of the words appear in all three books? As an extension activity, ask the children to compose orally two or three sentences that feature some of the words they have discussed. They could write out the best sentences.

Andrew Brodie: Improving Vocabulary for ages 10-11 © Bloomsbury Publishing Plc 2012

Word sorting: English, maths, science

Word Bank

sphere   spherical   prime   average

circuit   electricity   derivation   gravity   pair of compasses

habitat   micro-organism   digit   prefix   factor   experiment

median   biography   proverb   suffix   preposition   autobiography

paragraph   friction   magnetism   physics

probability   perimeter   perpendicular   dictionary   etymology

mnemonic   biology   biologist   chemistry

Look carefully at the words in the Word Bank. Which words could be found in an English book, which in a maths book and which in a science book? Write the words in the correct places below. Some of the words could appear in more than one book.

English Guide Book	Mathematics Explained	SCIENCE EVERY DAY

On a separate piece of paper, write three sentences using some of the vocabulary relating to English, maths or science.

Teacher's notes

Discuss the words above in relation to the category title cards from page 13. Do the children know what each word means? Can they think of any related words? For example, they could suggest the word 'electrical' in relation to the word 'electricity'. Ask the children to sort the words as though they appear in some non-fiction books: Could any of the words appear in more than one of the books? Could any of the words appear in all three books?

Word sorting:
English, maths, science

Name _____

Date _____

Look carefully at the words in the Word Bank. Which words could be found in an English book, which in a maths book and which in a science book? Write the words in the correct places below. Some of the words could appear in more than one book.

English Guide Book	Mathematics Explained	SCIENCE EVERY DAY

Find some more vocabulary for each book.

Teacher's notes

Discuss the words above in relation to the category title cards from page 13. Do the children know what each word means? To find extra vocabulary for each list, the children could research in the school library or on the internet. They could also consider searching for words related to those on the list: for example, the word 'biological' is clearly related to the word 'biology'. Can the children find any words that could appear in all three books? Can they explain how these words could be used in each context?

Andrew Brodie: Improving Vocabulary for ages 10-11 © Bloomsbury Publishing Plc 2012

Word sorting: machines, baking, flowers

Non-fiction

Information

Forces

Habitats

Health

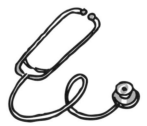

Teacher's notes

Photocopy and cut out the Non-fiction or Information headings and the category title cards to use in conjunction with the activities on the following three sheets. All of the vocabulary listed will be of great value to the pupils in their school work, now or in the future.

Word sorting: forces, habitat, health

gravity	newtons	pushing	pulling	attracting
repelling	opposing	friction	magnetism	measurement
adapted	mountains	rivers	moorland	water
desert	woodland	moisture	temperature	light
fitness	diet	exercise	medical	hospital
physical	nutrition	warmth	injury	stationary

Teacher's notes

Cut out the words and illustrations above and use them in conjunction with the category title cards from page 17. Ask the children to sort the words as though they appear in some school books: which words could be found in a book about forces, which in a book about habitats and which in a book about health? Could any of the words appear in more than one of the books? Could any of the words appear in all three books? As an extension activity, ask the children to compose orally two or three sentences that feature some of the words they have discussed. They could write out the best sentences.

Andrew Brodie: Improving Vocabulary for ages 10-11 © Bloomsbury Publishing Plc 2012

Word sorting:
forces, habitat, health

Name _____

Date _____

gravity   newtons   pushing   pulling   measurement

repelling   opposing   friction   magnetism   physical

desert   mountains   rivers   moorland   water

woodland   moisture   temperature   light

fitness   nutrition   diet   exercise   medical   hospital

warmth   attracting   adapted

acceleration   mechanical   aquatic   stationary   motion   ecological

environmental   conservation   humid   illness   species

geographical   injury   community

Look carefully at the words in the Word Bank. Which words could be found in a book about forces, which in a book about the habitats of birds or animals and which could be found in a book about health? Write the words in the correct places below. Some of the words could appear in more than one book.

Forces	Habitats	Staying Healthy

On a separate piece of paper, write three sentences using some of the vocabulary relating to forces, habitats and health.

Teacher's notes

Discuss the words above in relation to the category title cards from page 17. Do the children know what each word means? Can they think of any related words? For example, they could suggest the word 'nutritious' in relation to the word 'nutrition'. Ask the children to sort the words as though they appear in some non-fiction books: Could any of the words appear in more than one of the books? Could any of the words appear in all three books?

Word sorting:
forces, habitat, health

Name _____

Date _____

object
gravity   newtons   pushing   pulling   measurement
repelling   opposing   friction   magnetism   physical
desert   mountains   rivers   moorland   water
woodland   moisture   temperature   light
fitness
nutrition   diet   exercise   medical   hospital
warmth   attracting   adapted
acceleration
mechanical   aquatic   stationary   motion   ecological
environmental   conservation   humid   species
illness
velocity   geographical   injury   organism   community

Look carefully at the words in the Word Bank. Write the words in the correct book below. Some of the words could appear in more than one book.

Forces

_____ _____
_____ _____
_____ _____
_____ _____
_____ _____
_____ _____
_____ _____
_____ _____
_____ _____
_____ _____
_____ _____
_____ _____

Habitats

_____ _____
_____ _____
_____ _____
_____ _____
_____ _____
_____ _____
_____ _____
_____ _____
_____ _____
_____ _____
_____ _____
_____ _____

Staying Healthy

_____ _____
_____ _____
_____ _____
_____ _____
_____ _____
_____ _____
_____ _____
_____ _____
_____ _____
_____ _____
_____ _____
_____ _____

Find some more vocabulary for each book.

Teacher's notes

Discuss the words above in relation to the category title cards from page 17. Do the children know what each word means? To find extra vocabulary for each list, the children could research in the school library or on the internet. They could also consider searching for words related to those on the list: for example, the word 'adaptable' is clearly related to the word 'adapted'.

Word sorting: light, computers, structures

Non-fiction

Information

Light

Computers

Structures

Teacher's notes

Photocopy and cut out the Non-fiction or Information headings and the category title cards to use in conjunction with the activities on the following three sheets. Note that new vocabulary, or new uses of vocabulary, emerges continually in relation to computers: a 'tablet' computer simply did not exist a few years ago, for example.

Word sorting:
light, computers, structures

visible	source	speed	infrared	radiation
wavelength	ultraviolet	intensity	optical	program
memory	data	interface	digital	tablet
mobile	batteries	electronic	architecture	column
beam	truss	skeleton	bridge	tower
brace	joint	construction	bugs	storey

Teacher's notes

Cut out the words and illustrations above and use them in conjunction with the category title cards from page 21. Ask the children to sort the words as though they appear in some school books: which words could be found in a book about light, which in a book about computers and which in a book about structures? Could any of the words appear in more than one of the books? Could any of the words appear in all three books? As an extension activity, ask the children to compose orally two or three sentences that feature some of the words they have discussed. They could write out the best sentences.

Andrew Brodie: Improving Vocabulary for ages 10-11 © Bloomsbury Publishing Plc 2012

Word sorting: light, computers, structures

Name _____

Date _____

Word Bank

construction   wavelength   spectrum

binary   microprocessor   plant   bugs   operating system

brace   beam   truss   interface   bridge   tower

ultraviolet   intensity   optical   program

visible   commercial   source   skeleton   infrared   radiation

electronic   architecture   column

memory   batteries   data   speed   digital   tablet

mobile   joint   artificial intelligence   storey   aurora borealis

rainbow   residential   engineering   transparent

Look carefully at the words in the Word Bank. Which words could be found in a book about computers, which in a book about light and which in a book about structures? Write the words in the correct places below. Some of the words could appear in more than one book.

Learning about Light	Modern Computing	Building Structures
____ ____	____ ____	____ ____
____ ____	____ ____	____ ____
____ ____	____ ____	____ ____
____ ____	____ ____	____ ____
____ ____	____ ____	____ ____
____ ____	____ ____	____ ____
____ ____	____ ____	____ ____
____ ____	____ ____	____ ____

On a separate piece of paper, write three sentences using some of the vocabulary relating to light, computers and structures.

Teacher's notes

Discuss the words above in relation to the category title cards from page 21. Do the children know what each word means? Can they think of any related words? For example, they could suggest the word 'architectural' in relation to the word 'architecture'. Ask the children to sort the words as though they appear in some non-fiction books: Could any of the words appear in more than one of the books? Could any of the words appear in all three books?

Word sorting:
light, computers, structures

Name _____

Date _____

Word Bank

construction telescope input wavelength translucent spectrum

binary microprocessor plant interface bugs operating system

beam ultraviolet truss bridge tower

brace intensity pillar optical server program

visible commercial screen skeleton infrared radiation

reflection source electronic architecture column

memory batteries data wireless speed digital browsing tablet

mobile joint artificial intelligence storey aurora borealis

rainbow

function residential refraction engineering transparent touch

---

Look carefully at the words in the Word Bank. Write the words in the correct book below.
Some of the words could appear in more than one book.

Learning about Light	Modern Computing	Building Structures
_____ _____	_____ _____	_____ _____
_____ _____	_____ _____	_____ _____
_____ _____	_____ _____	_____ _____
_____ _____	_____ _____	_____ _____
_____ _____	_____ _____	_____ _____
_____ _____	_____ _____	_____ _____
_____ _____	_____ _____	_____ _____
_____ _____	_____ _____	_____ _____
_____ _____	_____ _____	_____ _____
_____ _____	_____ _____	_____ _____

Find some more vocabulary for each book.

Teacher's notes

Discuss the words above in relation to the category title cards from page 21. Do the children know what each word means? To find extra vocabulary for each list, the children could research in the school library or on the internet. They could also consider searching for words related to those on the list: for example, the word 'condensation' is clearly related to the word 'condensing'.

Andrew Brodie: Improving Vocabulary for ages 10-11 © Bloomsbury Publishing Plc 2012

Word sorting: electricity, music, history

Non-fiction

Information

Electricity

Music

History

Teacher's notes

Photocopy and cut out the Non-fiction or Ieformirtion headings and the category title cards to use in conjunction with the activities on the following three sheets. This categorisation activity can be very challenging for some children. It is important that they explain their choices when they are sorting the words - they may make some surprising decisions but ones that are perfectly valid.

Word sorting:
electricity, music, history

orchestra	band	notation	score	key
rhythm	beat	chord	tambourine	composer
generator	charge	current	electromagnet	connection
component	circuit	static	conductor	rain
ancient	exploration	heritage	archaeology	conqueror
Tudor	Victorian	mediaeval	ancestors	classical

Teacher's notes

Cut out the words and illustrations above and use them in conjunction with the category title cards from page 25. Ask the children to sort the words as though they appear in some school books: which words could be found in a book about electricity, which in a book about music and which in a book about history? Could any of the words appear in more than one of the books? Could any of the words appear in all three books? As an extension activity, ask the children to compose orally two or three sentences that feature some of the words they have discussed. They could write out the best sentences.

Andrew Brodie: Improving Vocabulary for ages 10-11 © Bloomsbury Publishing Plc 2012

Word sorting:
electricity, music, history

Name _____

Date _____

Word Bank

composer   melody   chord   ancient   rain

rhythm   archaeology   Anglo-Saxon

heritage

exploration   static   conqueror   Tudor

component   records   classical

orchestra   band   notation   score   key

Victorian   beat   ancestors   tambourine

generator   charge   current   electromagnet   connection

current   circuit   harmony   conductor

voltage   watts   power   alternating   Roman

theory   mediaeval   century   pitch

Look carefully at the words in the Word Bank. Which words could be found in a book about electricity, which in a book about music and which could be found in a book about history? Write the words in the correct places below. Some of the words could appear in more than one book.

Electricity	Music	History

On a separate piece of paper, write three sentences using some of the vocabulary relating to electricity, music or history.

Teacher's notes

Discuss the words above in relation to the category title cards from page 25. Do the children know what each word means? Can they think of any related words? For example, they could suggest the word 'composition' in relation to the word 'composer'. Ask the children to sort the words as though they appear in some non-fiction books: Could any of the words appear in more than one of the books? Could any of the words appear in all three books?

Word sorting:
electricity, music, history

Word Bank

composer instrumental melody ancient rain resistance
rhythm percussion siege chord Anglo-Saxon Tudor
exploration heritage archaeology conqueror energy
component records static classical serenade
orchestra band notation score lightning
Victorian opera armada ancestors tambourine beacon
generator transmission invasion electromagnet connection
current battle circuit current harmony conductor
voltage conductor charge power alternating Roman
key theory watts mediaeval beat century pitch woodwind

Look carefully at the words in the Word Bank. Write the words in the correct book below. Some of the words could appear in more than one book.

Electricity

_____ _____
_____ _____
_____ _____
_____ _____
_____ _____
_____ _____
_____ _____
_____ _____
_____ _____

Music

_____
_____
_____
_____
_____
_____
_____
_____
_____

History

_____ _____
_____ _____
_____ _____
_____ _____
_____ _____
_____ _____
_____ _____
_____ _____
_____ _____

Find some more vocabulary for each book.

Teacher's notes

Discuss the words above in relation to the category title cards from page 25. Do the children know what each word means? To find extra vocabulary for each list, the children could research in the school library or on the internet. They could also consider searching for words related to those on the list: for example, the word 'ancestral' is clearly related to the word 'ancestors'. Do the children notice that some words could appear in more than one of the lists? For example, the word 'conductor' could refer to material through which electricity can pass or to the person who directs an orchestra.

Andrew Brodie: Improving Vocabulary for ages 10-11 © Bloomsbury Publishing Plc 2012

Weather

Winter

Nouns

Adjectives

Comparative adjectives

Superlative adjectives

Verbs

Teacher's notes

Photocopy and cut out the Winter heading and the category cards to use in conjunction with the activities on the following three sheets. This activity provides lots of opportunities for speaking and listening and introduces important everyday vocabulary. Note that the grammatical terms listed above themselves form useful vocabulary.

Weather

rain	raining	rainy	rainier	rainiest
snow	snowing	snowy	snowier	snowiest
shining	sunny	sunnier	sunniest	shower
showery	blustery	wind	windy	windier
windiest	hurricane	gale	lightning	thunder
thundery	atmosphere	precipitation	depression	anticyclone

Teacher's notes

Cut out the words and illustrations above. Use the cards created from this sheet as prompts for discussion to ensure that this is a speaking and listening activity rather than a reading activity. Encourage the children to talk about today's weather and the weather over the past few days. Can the children create oral sentences using some of the verbs, nouns and adjectives? Talk about adjectives that make comparisons, giving examples in short sentences: Yesterday was rainy. Today is rainier. Tomorrow is likely to be the rainiest. Explain that the word 'rainier' is a comparative adjective and the word 'rainiest' is a superlative adjective. Discuss the fact that some of the adjectives can be made from nouns but some nouns do not have derivatives: for example the adjectives 'windy', 'windier' and 'windiest' can be derived from the noun 'wind' but no adjectives can be created directly from the noun 'lightning'.

Andrew Brodie: Improving Vocabulary for ages 10-11 © Bloomsbury Publishing Plc 2012

Weather

Name _____

Date _____

Word Bank

tornado   cloudy   wind   typhoon   rainiest

raining   sunny   climate   latitude   rainier   snowier   shower

rain   snow   blustery   snowing   snowy

shining   hurricane   sunnier   sunniest   anticyclone   windy

showery   precipitation   gale   lightning   thunder

windiest   atmosphere   depression   windy   tropical

snowiest   windier   thundery   moisture   jet stream

temperature   stormy

Write the words from the Word Bank in the appropriate places in the table.

Verbs	Nouns	Adjectives

Teacher's notes

Discuss the words in the Word Bank in conjunction with the category title cards from page 29. Ensure that this is firstly a speaking and listening activity although it will provide practice in both reading and writing. Can the children create oral sentences using some of the verbs, nouns and adjectives? Do they notice that there are fewer verbs than nouns or adjectives in the Word Bank? Talk about adjectives that make comparisons, giving examples in short sentences: Yesterday was quite sunny. Today is sunnier. Tomorrow is likely to be the sunniest. Explain that the word 'sunnier' is a comparative adjective and the word 'sunniest' is a superlative adjective. Discuss the fact that some of the adjectives can be made from nouns but some nouns do not have derivatives: for example the adjectives 'windy', 'windier' and 'windiest' can be derived from the noun 'wind' but no adjectives can be created directly from the noun 'lightning'.

Weather

Name _____

Date _____

Word Bank

tornado   cloudy   wind
                                                typhoon   rainiest
raining   sunny   climate   latitude
                                rainy   rainier
rain   blustery   snowy   snowier   shower
       snow   snowing
shining   sunnier   sunniest   anticyclone
           hurricane   windy
       showery
windiest   precipitation   gale   lightning   thunder
       atmosphere   depression
                            thundery   windy   tropical
snowiest   windier
   temperature   stormy   moisture   cyclone   jet stream
           monsoon

Write the verbs, nouns and the positive, comparative and superlative adjectives from the Word Bank in the appropriate places in the table. Can you think of extra words to write in the table?

Nouns		Verbs	Positive adjectives	Comparative adjectives	Superlative adjectives

Teacher's notes

Discuss the words in the Word Bank in conjunction with the category title cards from page 29. Ensure that this is firstly a speaking and listening activity although it will provide practice in both reading and writing. Can the children create oral sentences using some of the nouns, verbs and adjectives? Do they notice that there are fewer verbs than nouns or adjectives in the Word Bank? Talk about adjectives that make comparisons, giving examples in short sentences: Yesterday was quite sunny. Today is sunnier. Tomorrow is likely to be the sunniest. Explain that the word 'sunny' is called a positive adjective, the word 'sunnier' is a comparative adjective and the word 'sunniest' is a superlative adjective. Discuss the fact that some of the adjectives can be made from nouns but some nouns do not have derivatives: for example the adjectives 'windy', 'windier' and 'windiest' can be derived from the noun 'wind' but no adjectives can be created directly from the noun 'lightning'.

Andrew Brodie: Improving Vocabulary for ages 10-11 © Bloomsbury Publishing Plc 2012

Space

Space

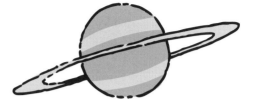

Nouns

Adjectives

Comparative adjectives

Superlative adjectives

Verbs

Teacher's notes

Photocopy and cut out the Space heading and the category cards to use in conjunction with the activities on the following three sheets. This activity provides lots of opportunities for speaking and listening and introduces important specialist vocabulary.

Space

planet	orbit	satellite	moon	solar system
universe	galaxy	Mercury	Venus	Earth
Mars	Jupiter	Saturn	Uranus	Neptune
terrestrial	gas giant	dwarf	asteroid	comet
gaseous	astronomy	exploration	mission	far
further	furthest	closer	closest	astronaut

Teacher's notes

Cut out the words and illustrations above. Use the cards created from this sheet as prompts for discussion to ensure that this is a speaking and listening activity as well as a reading activity. Encourage the children to talk about what they know about space. Discuss the 'terrestrial' planets, Mercury, Venus, Earth and Mars, which consist mainly of rock, and the 'gas giants', Jupiter, Saturn, Uranus and Neptune, which consist mainly of gaseous material. Can the children create oral sentences using some of the vocabulary? Talk about the adjectives that make comparisons, giving examples in short sentences: 'Mars is further away than the Earth from the sun', 'Neptune is the furthest planet from the sun'. (Note that Pluto is no longer classified as a planet by the International Astronomical Union but is instead considered to be a dwarf planet.) Explain that the word 'further' is a comparative adjective and the word 'furthest' is a superlative adjective. Note that the list includes the words 'closer' and 'closest' but not the word 'close'.

   Andrew Brodie: Improving Vocabulary for ages 10-11 © Bloomsbury Publishing Plc 2012

Space

Name _____

Date _____

Word Bank

spacewalk

interstellar

astronaut   furthest   Apollo   launcher   spacecraft

further   closest

gaseous   astronomy   exploration   mission   far

universe   Mercury   Venus

spaceflight   gas giant

terrestrial   dwarf   asteroid

planet   orbit   satellite   moon   solar system

galaxy   closer

Mars   Jupiter   Saturn   Uranus   Neptune

tourism   intergalactic

interplanetary

Earth   comet

Write five facts about space, using vocabulary from the Word Bank. You may need to research more information.

_____

_____

_____

_____

_____

Teacher's notes

Discuss the words in the Word Bank in conjunction with the category title cards from page 33. Ensure that this is firstly a speaking and listening activity although it will provide practice in both reading and writing. Encourage the children to talk about what they know about space. Discuss the 'terrestrial' planets, Mercury, Venus, Earth and Mars, which consist mainly of rock, and the 'gas giants', Jupiter, Saturn, Uranus and Neptune, which consist mainly of gaseous material. Can the children create oral sentences using some of the vocabulary? Talk about the adjectives that make comparisons, giving examples in short sentences: 'Mars is further away than the Earth from the sun', 'Neptune is the furthest planet from the sun'. (Note that Pluto is no longer classified as a planet by the International Astronomical Union but is instead considered to be a dwarf planet.) Explain that the word 'further' is a comparative adjective and the word 'furthest' is a superlative adjective. Note that the list includes the words 'closer' and 'closest' but not the word 'close'. You may wish to talk about science fiction, which has frequently featured interplanetary, interstellar and intergalactic space travel - this can be contrasted with the actual extent of human space travel.

Name _____

Date _____

Space

Word Bank

Earth   comet   spacecraft

astronaut   spacewalk   spacesuit   interstellar   launcher   cosmic   Apollo

further   furthest   radiation   closest

gaseous   astronomy   far   mission   weightless

exploration   Venus

universe   spaceflight   Mercury   dwarf   gas giant

terrestrial   orbit   asteroid

planet   satellite   solar system

Mars   tourism   galaxy   closer   moon

Jupiter   Saturn   Uranus   orientation   Neptune

interplanetary   gravity   weightlessness   atmosphere   intergalactic

Imagine that you are one of the first space tourists! Write about your journey into space, using some of the vocabulary from the Word Bank. You may need to research more information and to find more of the specialist vocabulary.

_____

_____

_____

_____

_____

_____

_____

_____

_____

_____

_____

_____

Teacher's notes

Discuss the words in the Word Bank in conjunction with the category title cards from page 33. Ensure that this is firstly a speaking and listening activity although it will provide practice in both reading and writing. Encourage the children to talk about what they know about space. Discuss the 'terrestrial' planets, Mercury, Venus, Earth and Mars, which consist mainly of rock, and the 'gas giants', Jupiter, Saturn, Uranus and Neptune, which consist mainly of gaseous material. Can the children create oral sentences using some of the vocabulary? You may wish to talk about science fiction, which has frequently featured interplanetary, interstellar and intergalactic space travel - this can be contrasted with the actual extent of human space travel. The development of space tourism gives the pupils the opportunity to talk about space in imaginary terms: what would it be like to travel in space? Note that current space tourism extends only to 'Low Earth Orbit'.

Andrew Brodie: Improving Vocabulary for ages 10-11 © Bloomsbury Publishing Plc 2012

Travel

Travel	Nouns 
Adjectives	Verbs

Teacher's notes

Photocopy and cut out the Travel heading and the category cards to use in conjunction with the activities on the following three sheets. This activity provides lots of opportunities for speaking and listening and introduces important everyday vocabulary. You may wish to extend the work to examine the spelling of some of the words.

Travel

traveller	tourist	vacation	holiday	relaxation
migration	emigration	immigration	commuting	transport
business	discovery	international	domestic	local
regional	itinerary	insurance	voyage	journey
adventure	hospitality	accommodation	flight	vehicle
aeroplane	traffic	passport	customs	foreign

Teacher's notes

Cut out the words and illustrations above and use them in conjunction with the category title cards from page 37. Use the cards created from this sheet as prompts for discussion to ensure that this is a speaking and listening activity rather than a reading activity. Encourage the children to talk about travelling. Point out that most of the words on the cards are nouns - can the children find related verbs? For example, 'travelling' is clearly related to 'traveller'. Which of the nouns do not have directly related verbs? For example, 'voyage'. Can the children identify the words that are not nouns?

Andrew Brodie: Improving Vocabulary for ages 10-11 © Bloomsbury Publishing Plc 2012

Travel

Name _____

Date _____

Word Bank

emigration   commuting

tourist   vacation   holiday   adventure

traveller   itinerary   accommodation   voyage
     vehicle

migration   international   domestic   relaxation

discovery   immigration

business   journey
     hospitality   aeroplane   flight   local
regional   insurance   transport

Which of the words in the Word Bank are adjectives?

_____ _____ _____ _____

The other words in the Word Bank are nouns. Try to find a verb that is related to each noun. Write your pairs of words on the lines below.

_____	_____	_____	_____
_____	_____	_____	_____
_____	_____	_____	_____
_____	_____	_____	_____
_____	_____	_____	_____
_____	_____	_____	_____
_____	_____	_____	_____
_____	_____	_____	_____

Teacher's notes

Discuss the words in the Word Bank in conjunction with the category title cards from page 37. Ensure that this is firstly a speaking and listening activity although it will provide practice in both reading and writing. Encourage the children to talk about travelling. Point out that most of the words on the cards are nouns - can the children find related verbs? For example, 'accommodate' is clearly related to 'accommodation'. Which of the nouns do not have directly related verbs? For example, 'voyage'. Can the children identify the words that are not nouns?

Travel

Name _____

Date _____

Word Bank

temporary   commuting

emigration   tourist   vacation   holiday   adventure

traveller   itinerary   accommodation   voyage

vehicle

migration   international   domestic   relaxation

navigate   immigration   volunteer

discovery   local

business   journey

hospitality   aeroplane   flight

regional   continental   insurance   transport

Write a short story about a journey you could make. Your task is to use appropriately as many of the words in the Word Bank as possible!

_____

_____

_____

_____

_____

_____

_____

_____

_____

_____

_____

_____

_____

Teacher's notes

Discuss the words in the Word Bank in conjunction with the category title cards from page 37. Ensure that this is firstly a speaking and listening activity although it will provide practice in both reading and writing. Encourage the children to talk about travelling. Point out that most of the words on the cards are nouns - can the children find related verbs? For example, 'discover' is clearly related to 'discovery'. Which of the nouns do not have directly related verbs? For example, 'voyage'. Can the children identify the words that are not nouns?

Andrew Brodie: Improving Vocabulary for ages 10-11 © Bloomsbury Publishing Plc 2012

Food

Food

Nouns

Adjectives

Comparative
adjectives

Superlative
adjectives

Verbs

Teacher's notes

Photocopy and cut out the Food heading and the category cards to use in conjunction with the activities
on the following three sheets.

Food

| greedy | greedier | greediest | nutrition | nutritious |

| sustenance | provisions | groceries | greengrocer | delicatessen |

| scoff | consume | consumption | dessert | lunch |

| dinner | supper | breakfast | gobble | dine |

| taste | tasty | tastier | tastiest | course |

| appetite | appetizer | favourite | least favourite | vitamins |

Teacher's notes

Cut out the words and illustrations above and use them in conjunction with the category title cards from page 41, pointing out that some of the vocabulary is no longer fashionable. Use the cards created from this sheet as prompts for discussion to ensure that this is a speaking and listening activity rather than a reading activity. Encourage the children to talk about favourite foods and foods that they don't like. Can they create oral sentences about food using some of the nouns, verbs and adjectives? Can they find the comparative and superlative adjectives?

Andrew Brodie: Improving Vocabulary for ages 10-11 © Bloomsbury Publishing Plc 2012

Name _____

Date _____

Word Bank

starters   nutritional   greediest   nutrition   fats

sustenance   provisions   carbohydrates   minerals   dessert   delicacy   lunch

dinner   tasty   consume   consumption   greengrocer   delicatessen

supper   greedy   tastier

dietary   scoff   groceries   nutritious   dine   course

appetizer   vitamins   gobble   proteins

breakfast   allergies

appetite   taste   greedier   favourite   least favourite   tastiest

greedily   nutrients

Write the words from the Word Bank in the appropriate places in the table.

Nouns	Verbs	Adjectives

Which word in the Word Bank is an adverb? _____

Teacher's notes

Discuss the words in the Word Bank in conjunction with the category title cards from page 41, pointing out that some of the vocabulary is no longer fashionable. Ensure that this is firstly a speaking and listening activity although it will provide practice in both reading and writing. Encourage the children to talk about their favourite and least favourite foods. Ask them to look at the words in the Word Bank very carefully: can they find the verbs, nouns, positive adjectives (greedy), comparative adjectives (greedier) and superlative adjectives (greediest)? Do they notice the adverb greedily, which could be used to describe how someone is eating?

Food

Name _____

Date _____

Word Bank

starters   nutritional   carbohydrates   greediest   nutrition   fats

sustenance   provisions   glucose   minerals   delicacy

dinner   tasty   consume   consumption   dessert   sucrose

supper   greedy   lunch   greengrocer   delicatessen

scoff

dietary   groceries   tastier   nutritious   course

appetite   appetizer   vitamins   gobble   dine

taste   breakfast   proteins

greedily   greedier   favourite   agriculture   allergies

tastiest

fructose   nutrients   vegetarian   least favourite   production

Pick five words from the Word Bank that are new to you. Research the five words and write a definition for each one.

_____

_____

_____

_____

_____

_____

_____

_____

_____

_____

_____

Teacher's notes

Discuss the words in the Word Bank in conjunction with the category title cards from page 41. Ensure that this is firstly a speaking and listening activity although it will provide practice in both reading and writing. Encourage the children to talk about their favourite and least favourite foods. Ask them to look at the words in the Word Bank very carefully: can they find the verbs, nouns, positive adjectives (greedy), comparative adjectives (greedier) and superlative adjectives (greediest)? Do they notice the adverb greedily, which could be used to describe how someone is eating?

   Andrew Brodie: Improving Vocabulary for ages 10-11 © Bloomsbury Publishing Plc 2012

Cooking

Cooking

Nouns

Adjectives

Comparative adjectives

Superlative adjectives

Verbs

Teacher's notes

Photocopy and cut out the Cooking heading and the category cards to use in conjunction with the activities on the following three sheets.

method	cookery	recipe	cuisine	sweetness	saltiness
healthy	healthier	healthiest	frying	grilling	poaching
boiling	roasting	simmering	preparing	basting	baking
texture	taste	Italian	Chinese	Indian	Thai
flavour	combination	prefer	mixing	blending	heating
microwave	barbecue	salty	saltier	saltiest	ingredients

Teacher's notes

Cut out the words and illustrations above and use them in conjunction with the category title cards from page 45. Use the cards created from this sheet as prompts for discussion to ensure that this is a speaking and listening activity rather than a reading activity. This Key Activity is closely related to the previous one about food. Encourage the children to talk about who does the cooking at home, what cooking they have done themselves, what type of cooking they like, etc. Can they create oral sentences about cooking using some of the nouns, verbs and adjectives? Can they find the comparative and superlative adjectives?

Andrew Brodie: Improving Vocabulary for ages 10-11 © Bloomsbury Publishing Plc 2012

Cooking

Word Bank

prefer saltiness   baking   Thai
healthy   restaurant   recipe   convection   cuisine   salty   ingredients
boiling   saltiest   processor   preserves   preparing   sweetness
combination   cookery   simmering   healthiest   Chinese   blending
texture   taste   frying   method   Indian
flavour   roasting   Italian   mixing   basting
microwave   induction   poaching   healthily   barbecue
heating   healthier   saltier   sushi   grilling

Write the words from the Word Bank in the appropriate places in the table.

Nouns	Verbs	Adjectives

Which word in the Word Bank is an adverb? _____

Teacher's notes

Discuss the words in the Word Bank in conjunction with the category title cards from page 45, pointing out that some of the vocabulary is no longer fashionable. Ensure that this is firstly a speaking and listening activity although it will provide practice in both reading and writing. This Key Activity is closely related to the previous one about food. Encourage the children to talk about who does the cooking at home, what cooking they have done themselves, what type of cooking they like, etc. Can they create oral sentences about cooking using some of the nouns, verbs and adjectives? Some of the words are both nouns and verbs: e.g. microwave and barbecue. Can they find the comparative and superlative adjectives and the single adverb in the Word Bank?

Cooking

Name _____

Date _____

Word Bank

method   combination
recipe   mixing   cookery   gastronomy   healthily   flavour
prefer   induction   cuisine
        blending   poaching   sweetness   saltier
              sushi   roasting
frying   grilling   healthier   preserves   texture   preparing
        healthy   Chinese   taste
microwave   salty   processor
convection   ingredients   Thai   blanching
                        barbecue   saltiness
simmering
              braising   sanitizing   searing   restaurant
basting   technique   Indian   boiling
                    Italian
saltiest   heating   baking   contamination   healthiest

Pick five words from the Word Bank that are new to you. Research the five words and write a definition for each one.

_____

_____

_____

_____

_____

_____

_____

_____

_____

_____

Teacher's notes

Discuss the words in the Word Bank in conjunction with the category title cards from page 45. Ensure that this is firstly a speaking and listening activity although it will provide practice in both reading and writing. This Key Activity is closely related to the previous one about food. Encourage the children to talk about who does the cooking at home, what cooking they have done themselves, what type of cooking they like, etc. Can they create oral sentences about cooking using some of the nouns, verbs and adjectives? Some of the words are both nouns and verbs: e.g. microwave and barbecue. Can they find the comparative and superlative adjectives and the single adverb in the Word Bank?

Andrew Brodie: Improving Vocabulary for ages 10-11 © Bloomsbury Publishing Plc 2012

Word sorting: mountains, rivers, coasts

Non-fiction

Information

Mountains

Rivers

Coasts

Teacher's notes

Photocopy and cut out the Non-fiction or Information headings and the category cards to use in conjunction with the activities on the following three sheets. This categorisation activity can be very challenging for some children. They are likely to need some of the specialist vocabulary when working on geography now or in the future.

Word sorting: mountains, rivers, coasts

range	summit	peak	elevation	altitude	mountainous
mountaineering	skiing	hiking	volcano	eruption	magma
plateau	erosion	tree-line	source	mouth	delta
tributary	freshwater	floodplain	estuary	precipitation	meander
irrigation	hydroelectric	shore	gulf	bay	cliffs
fjord	inlet	landscape	beach	marsh	harbour

Teacher's notes

Cut out the words and illustrations above and use them in conjunction with the category title cards from page 49. Ask the children to sort the words as though they appear in some non-fiction books: which words could be found in a book about mountains, which in a book about rivers and which could be found in a book about coasts? Encourage the children to consider whether the words could appear in more than one of the books. Could any of the words appear in all three books? As an extension activity, ask the children to compose orally two or three sentences that feature some of the words they have discussed. They could write out the best sentences.

Andrew Brodie: Improving Vocabulary for ages 10-11 © Bloomsbury Publishing Plc 2012

Word sorting: mountains, rivers, coasts

Name _____

Date _____

Look carefully at the words in the Word Bank. Which words could be found in a book about mountains, which in a book about rivers and which could be found in a book about coasts? Write the words in the correct places below. Some of the words could appear in more than one book. You may like to add some extra words.

Mountains

_____ _____
_____ _____
_____ _____
_____ _____
_____ _____
_____ _____
_____ _____

Rivers

_____ _____
_____ _____
_____ _____
_____ _____
_____ _____
_____ _____
_____ _____

Coasts

_____ _____
_____ _____
_____ _____
_____ _____
_____ _____
_____ _____
_____ _____

On a separate piece of paper, write three sentences using some of the vocabulary relating to mountains, rivers or coasts.

Teacher's notes

Discuss the words above in relation to the category title cards from page 49. Do the children know what each word means? Can they think of any related words? Ask the children to sort the words as though they appear in some non-fiction books: Could any of the words appear in more than one of the books? Could any of the words appear in all three books?

Word sorting: mountains, rivers, coasts

Name _____

Date _____

orography eruption mountainous summit gulf hiking

elevation landscape harbour skiing tree-line

volcano mouth magma plateau erosion surface

weathered precipitation delta tributary headland floodplain lake

estuary bay cliffs meander lagoon irrigation freshwater shore

glaciation hydroelectric

snowboarding volcanic mangrove drainage landform

inlet oxbow

potamology whitewater sand-dunes mountaineering hydrological channel

altitude beach fjord range marsh peak

watercourse

Pick five words from the Word Bank that are new to you. Research the five words and write a definition for each one.

_____

_____

_____

_____

_____

_____

_____

_____

_____

_____

_____

Teacher's notes

Discuss the words above in relation to the category title cards from page 49. Do the children know what each word means? Can they think of any related words? Ask the children to sort the words according to whether they are related to mountains, rivers or coasts - they could highlight the words to colour code them but will need to be aware that some words could be sorted into one, two or all three categories.

Andrew Brodie: Improving Vocabulary for ages 10-11 © Bloomsbury Publishing Plc 2012

Word sorting: drama, poetry, art

Non-fiction	Fiction
Information	Entertainment
 Drama	 Poetry
 Art	

Teacher's notes

Photocopy and cut out the Non-fiction or Fiction headings and the category cards to use in conjunction with the activities on the following three sheets. This categorisation activity can be very challenging for some children. You may like to find some examples of the different types of poem that are listed.

Word sorting: drama, poetry, art

audience	dramatic	comedy	tragedy	performance	dialogue
improvisation	pantomime	character	playwright	mystery	theatrical
opera	verse	rhyme	rhythm	scan	alliteration
onomatopoeia	haiku	narrative	limerick	nonsense	decorative
drawing	photography	painting	sculpture	printmaking	impressionism
graffiti	script	stanza	couplet	narrative	

Teacher's notes

Cut out the words and illustrations above and use them in conjunction with the category title cards from page 53. Ask the children to sort the words as though they appear in some books: which words could be found in a book about drama, which in a book about poetry and which could be found in a book about art? Could any of the words appear in more than one of the books? Could any of the words appear in all three books? You may like to give the children some examples of onomatopoeia: moo, hiss, woof, etc. As an extension activity, ask the children to compose orally two or three sentences that feature some of the words they have discussed. They could write out the best sentences.

Word sorting: drama, poetry, art

Name _____

Date _____

Look carefully at the words in the Word Bank. Which words could be found in a book about drama, which in a book about poetry and which could be found in a book about art? Write the words in the correct places below. Some of the words could appear in more than one book. You may like to add some extra words.

Drama	Poetry	Art

On a separate piece of paper, write three sentences using some of the specialist vocabulary related to drama, poetry or art.

Teacher's notes

Discuss the words above in relation to the category title cards from page 53. Do the children know what each word means? Can they think of any related words? For example, they could suggest the word 'improvised' in relation to the word 'improvisation'. Ask the children to sort the words as though they appear in some books: Could any of the words appear in more than one of the books? Could any of the words appear in all three books?

Word sorting: drama, poetry, art

Name _____

Date _____

Pick five words from the Word Bank that are new to you. Research the five words and write a definition for each one.

_____

_____

_____

_____

_____

_____

_____

_____

_____

Teacher's notes

Discuss the words above in relation to the category title cards from page 53. Do the children know what each word means? Ask the children to sort the words according to whether they are related to drama, poetry or art - they could highlight the words to colour code them but will need to be aware that some words could be sorted into one, two or all three categories.

 Andrew Brodie: Improving Vocabulary for ages 10-11 © Bloomsbury Publishing Plc 2012

Ambitions

Ambitions

Education

Occupations

The future

Teacher's notes

Photocopy and cut out these category title cards to use in conjunction with the activities on the following three sheets. This activity introduces a range of vocabulary all relating to the pupils' future lives. They may well be able to think of other words, which reflect their personal ambitions.

Ambitions

adulthood	employment	secondary
school	education	university
college	working	earning
qualifying	qualifications	studying
participating	professional	occupation
relaxing	health	engineering
professions	entertainment	media
construction	manufacturing	agriculture
sport	career	environment
travel	sales	marketing
technology	finance	hospitality

Teacher's notes

Cut out the words and illustrations above and use them in conjunction with the category title cards from page 57. Use the cards created from this sheet as prompts for discussion to ensure that this is a speaking and listening activity rather than a reading activity. Encourage the children to talk about their ambitions for the future: what are their ambitions for their secondary school life, their education beyond school, and their roles as adults? Do they know what all of the words mean? They could sort the words according to whether they relate to life before or after the completion of education. They could also identify examples of jobs that could be classified under the career headings provided. Can they think of any other career headings?

 Andrew Brodie: Improving Vocabulary for ages 10-11 © Bloomsbury Publishing Plc 2012

Ambitions

Name _____

Date _____

Word Bank

adulthood professions sport qualifying carpenter health shop assistant

university accountant cowherd studying secondary nurse

recycling operative college sales driver solicitor media footballer

relaxing

earning employment construction career school

technology

car designer professional marketing agriculture engineering writer travel

chef working manufacturing teacher advertising agent hospitality

machinist participating environment entertainment qualifications

architect occupation computer programmer finance education singer

Look carefully at the words in the Word Bank. Find the career headings and an example of a career that belongs with that heading. The first one is done for you.

Career Heading	Example
health	nurse

Teacher's notes

Discuss the words in the Word Bank in conjunction with the category title cards from page 57. Ensure that this is firstly a speaking and listening activity although it will provide practice in both reading and writing. Encourage the children to talk about their ambitions for the future: what are their ambitions for their secondary school life, their education beyond school, and their roles as adults? They could consider their personal and family lives as well as their careers. The writing task should be completed after the children have discussed all the words, researching any words that are new to them.

Ambitions

Name _____

Date _____

Word Bank

adulthood   professions   sport   qualifying   carpenter   health   shop assistant
university   accountant   cowherd   studying   secondary   nurse
recycling operative   college   relaxing   sales   driver   solicitor   media   footballer
earning   employment   technology   construction   career   school
car designer   professional   marketing   agriculture   engineering   writer   travel
chef   working   manufacturing   teacher   advertising agent   hospitality
machinist   participating   environment   entertainment   qualifications
architect   occupation   computer programmer   finance   education   singer

Write about your ambitions for the future. Use some of the vocabulary from the Word Bank.

_____

_____

_____

_____

_____

_____

_____

_____

_____

_____

_____

_____

_____

_____

_____

_____

Teacher's notes

Discuss the words in the Word Bank in conjunction with the category title cards from page 57. Ensure that this is firstly a speaking and listening activity although it will provide practice in both reading and writing. Encourage the children to talk about their ambitions for the future: what are their ambitions for their secondary school life, their education beyond school, and their roles as adults? They could consider their personal and family lives as well as their careers. The writing task should be completed after the children have discussed all the words, researching any words that are new to them.

Andrew Brodie: Improving Vocabulary for ages 10-11 © Bloomsbury Publishing Plc 2012

Jabberwocky

’Twas brillig, and the slithy toves
Did gyre and gimble in the wabe;
All mimsy were the borogoves,
And the mome raths outgrabe.

“Beware the Jabberwock, my son!
The jaws that bite, the claws that catch!
Beware the Jubjub bird, and shun
The frumious Bandersnatch!”

He took his vorpal sword in hand:
Long time the manxome foe he sought—
So rested he by the Tumtum tree,
And stood awhile in thought.

And as in uffish thought he stood,
The Jabberwock, with eyes of flame,
Came whiffling through the tulgey wood,
And burbled as it came!

One, two! One, two! and through and through
The vorpal blade went snicker-snack!
He left it dead, and with its head
He went galumphing back.

“And hast thou slain the Jabberwock?
Come to my arms, my beamish boy!
O frabjous day! Callooh! Callay!”
He chortled in his joy.

’Twas brillig, and the slithy toves
Did gyre and gimble in the wabe;
All mimsy were the borogoves,
And the mome raths outgrabe.

Lewis Carroll

Teacher's notes

Display the poem for the pupils to see clearly. Point out that it is written as quatrain verses and that each verse contains 'nonsense' words: Lewis Carroll invented his own vocabulary for the poem, which when mixed with 'real' words, helps the reader or listener to imagine what is happening.

Jabberwocky

Name _____

Date _____

Read these two verses of Jabberwocky.

'Twas brillig, and the slithy toves
Did gyre and gimble in the wabe;
All mimsy were the borogoves,
And the mome raths outgrabe.

"Beware the Jabberwock, my son!
The jaws that bite, the claws that catch!
Beware the Jubjub bird, and shun
The frumious Bandersnatch!"

Which 'nonsense' words in the verses could be the names of animals or birds?

_____   _____   _____   _____

_____   _____

Can you make up your own nonsense name for an animal or bird?

_____

Teacher's notes

Give each pupil a copy of this sheet featuring the first two verses of the nonsense poem Jabberwocky. Read the verses through with them, several times if necessary, and encourage them to read the verses out loud before asking them to underline or highlight the words that they don't know. Talk these through with them, explaining any 'real' words and asking them if they can work out what the 'nonsense' words could possibly represent.

Jabberwocky

Name _____

Date _____

Read these two verses of Jabberwocky.

He took his vorpal sword in hand:
Long time the manxome foe he sought—
So rested he by the Tumtum tree,
And stood awhile in thought.

And as in uffish thought he stood,
The Jabberwock, with eyes of flame,
Came whiffling through the tulgey wood,
And burbled as it came!

Which 'nonsense' words in the verses are adjectives?

_____ _____ _____ _____

Which of the nonsense words is a verb?

_____

Write a sentence that includes a made-up noun, verb and adjective.

_____

_____

Teacher's notes

Give each pupil a copy of this sheet featuring two verses of the nonsense poem Jabberwocky. Read the verses through with them, several times if necessary, and encourage them to read the verses out loud before asking them to underline or highlight the words that they don't know. Talk these through with them, explaining any 'real' words and asking them if they can work out what the 'nonsense' words could possibly represent.

Name _____

Date _____

Read these three verses of Jabberwocky.

One, two! One, two! and through and through
The vorpal blade went snicker-snack!
He left it dead, and with its head
He went galumphing back.

"And hast thou slain the Jabberwock?
Come to my arms, my beamish boy!
O frabjous day! Callooh! Callay!"
He chortled in his joy.

'Twas brillig, and the slithy toves
Did gyre and gimble in the wabe;
All mimsy were the borogoves,
And the mome raths outgrabe.

Find four 'nonsense' adjectives.

_____   _____   _____   _____

Find two nonsense verbs.   _____   _____

Find five nonsense nouns.   _____   _____   _____

_____   _____

Make up your own quatrain verse, which features some made-up vocabulary.

_____

_____

_____

_____

Teacher's notes

Give each pupil a copy of this sheet featuring the final three verses of the nonsense poem Jabberwocky. Encourage them to read the verses out loud before asking them to underline or highlight the words that they don't know. Talk these through with them, explaining any 'real' words and asking them if they can work out what the 'nonsense' words could possibly represent. Note that the word 'galumphing' was invented by Lewis Carroll but is now in popular use.

Andrew Brodie: Improving Vocabulary for ages 10-11 © Bloomsbury Publishing Plc 2012